ISBN 9781527295186

Images: I have gone to great lengths to establish copyright of the images and to credit them appropriately and apologise if any errors have occurred.

Cover design and original oil painting by Terry Grace

Back cover: The Silver Star Garage at Porton Down in 1927

Printed by Amesbury Print Centre

Catkin Books 2021

DEDICATION AND ACKNOWLEDGEMENTS

I would like to dedicate this book to Jack Parsons, without whom, the memory of Silver Star would be that much more distant. Together with much help and encouragement from his late wife Sherry, Jack restored two of the firms' vehicles which has allowed us to once again catch an occasional glimpse of what life was like in the Bourne Valley back in the 1950s and 1960s. The daunting task of restoring such vehicles and returning them to their pristine condition is more than a labour of love, it is a great contribution to our history, and one for which we should be most grateful.

There are still a few local people around who remember fondly this unique bus service, but without these tangible reminders, the legend of Silver Star may have fallen into the depth of time and been forgotten, as so many of the contemporary companies have. I am very grateful too for Jack's generous contribution of photographs and detailed knowledge of the vehicles, the staff and the business that was Silver Star.

I would also like to acknowledge the help and photographs of all that have allowed me to use them in this book. I am particularly grateful to Dave Mant who so kindly sent me many pictures which have been used here. Also, to Mary Dixon who was particularly helpful.

In memory of my late father-in-law David Short who was an enthusiast of local bus companies, and who was looking forward to seeing this book published but sadly didn't quite make it.

Silver Star Motor Services

of Porton Down

Introduction

It is important to start off with the fact that I am not a bus expert and know very little about them, so any information on specifications is gathered from the literature and other sources and in many respects is not what this book is about. So, saying, I have learnt quite a lot about the Silver Star fleet in researching this book, and for the bus enthusiast have included a pictorial history. I am though nostalgic for this bus service which served the two villages I grew up in, namely Gomeldon and Porton.

The history of the Silver Star Motor Services has been addressed before but never I think in a single volume, most of the available information coming from old magazine articles and the odd chapter in books.

So, I intend to get as much information as possible into one volume, and concentrate not just on the vehicles, but also reminiscences of the service, and the staff which made this company so memorable.

History of Silver Star Motor Services

I have included this short history in order to get the information into the public domain where it belongs and to get the available information on Silver Star into one easily accessible volume. There was a series of short articles about Silver Star in the 1960s and there have been short chapters in other bus-related volumes. The magazine articles are a little difficult to come by. I have been asked by the author not to provide a reference to him or the articles, so have respected that and not detailed his name in the bibliography.

In the beginning

It was in September 1923 that school friends E. W. Shergold and B. F. White started their bus service from Porton Down to Salisbury. The two young men purchased a new Model T Ford chassis and had built on it a 14-seat aluminium bus body. According to most sources, the body was made by Pitt and Sons of Fordingbridge. However, there is some record of the body possibly originating from Heaver's of Durrington. In "Coachwork by Heaver" by John Carman and Kathy Garland, we learn that H. N. Pitt of Amesbury, trading as Pitson, was known to sell Heaver bodies. What is not known is whether he sold such bodies to his brother aka Pitt & Sons of Fordingbridge. An interesting suggestion, but no actual proof. There seems to be little or no information on Pitt and sons of Fordingbridge.

The photo above shows a proud Eddie Shergold in front of HR 9447, The first Silver Star vehicle. (Peter Daniels Collection)

I can't imagine that vehicle carrying 14 passengers, I guess it never attempted Gomeldon Hill?

It has always been suggested that the name Silver Star came from a popular Waltz of that time and this may be the case, but I wonder if the shiny polished aluminium of this vehicle was also instrumental in their choice of name for the company. Peter Gould in his account of the company suggests that Eddie Shergold's time on the destroyer "Morning Star" may also have played a part in the naming.

Apparently, the service was on a daily basis from the onset and timed to coincide with schools and the workforce at Porton Down.

There was always competition for Silver Star, most notably that Of Armstead from Newton Toney, but also some other small concerns and of course Wilts and Dorset who were also expanding their fleet and routes at that time.

The wonderful picture on the following page shows the Silver Star fleet and staff in 1927 at Porton Down. Note the 6-wheel Rolls-Royce chassis, being one of two that they were to modify and have rebuilt as buses. Also, the HR 9447 is not present, so possibly was too underpowered for the fleet.

(Author photo from Gillard Collection)

From left to right, RR converted 6-wheel chassis prior to being bodied, Crossley B9396, Albion Viking MR 8049, Albion Viking ML 1862, Crossley BY 6412.

Note the headboards with the star logo, the star first appeared as an eight-pointed device, later to a five-point star and was never silver but in fact white

This building has been described as an ex-aeroplane shed but in fact, that was much later in the early 1950s. At only 25ft wide it would not have been suitable as an aeroplane shed.

(By counting the corrugations on the front of the shed, it is possible to calculate the width, since each corrugation is 3" from the next in standard sheets of this material at the time. By this calculation, the shed is indeed 25ft wide.

In the following map of the site in 1917, we can see that the building was a store for Porton Camp with possibly a concrete apron around it. From the scale on this map, the store was 9 metres wide which is equivalent to ca 25ft. I suspect therefore that it is the very same building, and that Silver Star managed to purchase that building sometime after the first world war when the chemical warfare research activities declined for a time and the store was surplus to requirements. The building together with the associated land was leased to Shergold and White. In 1946 when the lease was renewed with the War Department, the rent was set at £30 per annum.

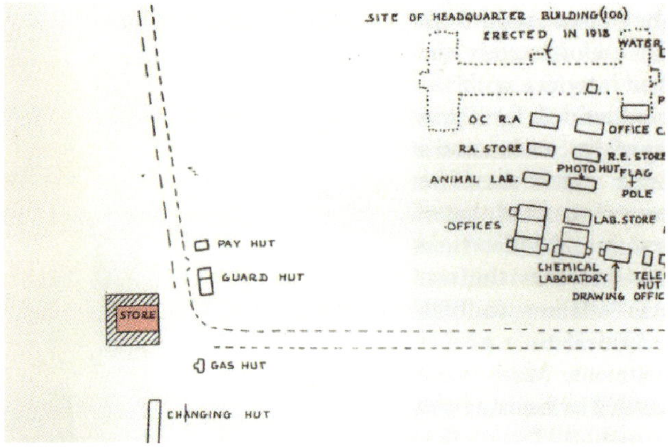

1917 map of the site which was to become Silver Star Garage.

.

The following is a picture of the Rolls-Royce X 2500 after having the body fitted.

(Author collection, unknown)

And a side view:

(Author collection; Gillard)

According to the Bus Fleet List, both Rolls-Royce chassis were converted to 6 wheelers. There seems to be little evidence as to the reason for this strange-looking arrangement, and it was never used on any of their other bus chassis.

I have been told that this 6-wheel arrangement was considered unorthodox and somewhat dangerous by the Rolls-Royce company, and in fact that they refused to associate themselves with it, and would not have serviced it, even if asked to do so.

Interesting to note that turning Rolls-Royce chassis into 6-wheel buses was not unique to Silver Star as the following picture of a similar vehicle in Libya shows:

In addition to the two Rolls-Royce vehicles, two Crossley ex-RAF tenders were purchased and rebodied by Pitts of Fordingbridge. One was given a saloon type body, and the other a 14-seat open tourer body and both were presented in the polished aluminium livery.

The following two pictures show these two vehicles:

Crossley B9396 from 1924 and as seen second from left in the garage picture shown previously. Note the eight-pointed star emblem. (Author's collection; Gillard)

Crossley BY 6412 (Peter Daniels Collection)

(Gillard collection)

Leyland TS MW 4774 delivered new to Silver Star in 1929 and seen here outside the Salisbury Guildhall. Note the "S&W" motif in addition to the "Silver Star" Logo and also the stars on the wheels. (Gillard Collection)

In 1930 The Road Traffic Act meant that bus companies had to apply for licences to trade on certain routes. Silver Star applied to operate from Allington to Salisbury via their base at Porton Down, from Salisbury to Sling Camp (an annexe to Bulford) and Amesbury. Also, from Salisbury to Andover including Amesbury Tidworth and Ludgershall.

With the exception of the Andover to Salisbury route, the licences were all granted. By 1933 Silver Star had taken over some licences of other small companies, and this included excursion licences from Bulford Camp.

MW8981

In 1931 the company bought an AEC Regal MW8981 and A Leyland TS1 MW8982.

The following picture is of the Skylark Bus Company from Woodfalls, south of Salisbury. MW8981 is said to be the 6th bus from right, so assume they bought it from Silver Star?

1932 was not a good year for Eddie Shergold and Silver Star. Eddie was involved in a car accident at Abbott's Ann, in which he managed to overturn his car whilst attempting to avoid an oncoming motorist. Both cars had the intention of passing a horse and cart, but Eddie skidded on a wet and greasy road resulting in the crash. His passenger Louis Smith of St Thomas's Bridge Salisbury died in the accident. Louis Smith was employed by Silver Star as an Inspector. The inquest jury returned a verdict of "accidental death"

In 1934, Silver Star purchased WV5823 which was a Leyland LT5A with a Burlingham body. The following rare picture shows that vehicle, outside the original garage at Porton Down

(Courtesy Jack Parsons)

In 1938, Silver Star bought TR5945 from Hants and Dorset which was a Leyland PLSC3 which they used for some time but was later converted to half lorry body style as in the following picture. It was used in that form until 1952. But it was also equipped with a crane later in life and used to erect the aeroplane hangar which came from Ashford, Kent. (see later)

TR5945 (Unknown)

Just prior to WW2 there was a substantial increase in business due to the Military Camps such as Larkhill and Figsbury emerging in preparation for war.

(Unknown)

This strange but charismatic vehicle seen here in Salisbury was bought by Silver Star in 1936. It originally had a "half-cab" (i.e., a small single cab for the driver), but was converted to the "full front" version by Heaver Coach Builders of Durrington. This bus was the only vehicle returned to Silver Star after the wartime requisitioning.

(J S Cockshott Archive, The Transport Library) .

In order to accommodate the increase in trade, the company bought six double-decker buses in 1939. These were Leyland TD1s purchased from Yorkshire Woollen District, with registration numbers HD 4153-4158.

Throughout the war, Silver Star supplemented their partly requisitioned fleet with a collection of elderly vehicles acquired from various sources. They also lost another of their vehicles when it was in collision with a tank at Targett's Corner, Porton. (This may have been MW4774 seen in a previous picture, or Leyland MW5885 of which there seems to be no photographs)

HD 4154 in Blue Boar Row Salisbury (Author collection, unknown)

HD4156 in Blue Boar Row sometime before 1950 when it was withdrawn from service. (unknown)

And in the following picture, HD4155 in Salisbury, after having been rebodied in 1949 (Courtesy Brian Botley):

In 1940 Silver Star bought two ex-Tilling Stevens buses which looked quite antiquated even for that time, and it is supposed that they had to acquire anything they could get their hands on in that Wartime period.

UF4659 (Tilling-Stevens) is shown abandoned, possibly at Porton in the following rather poor image (post-war).

(Unknown)

And UF5076:

(Unknown)

After the war during which time many of their vehicles had been requisitioned for the war effort, the Silver Star Company was in a less than healthy situation, with a collection of mainly worn-out buses.

In 1945, the company purchased a Leyland tiger TS7 coach which came from the US Army depot at Weyhill and is shown in the following photo.

Like AAM756 (shown previously), this vehicle was also rebodied by Heaver's of Durrington in 1953.

BMX 331 after the Heaver rebuild (1953), Tidworth? (Courtesy D. Clark)

In general Heaver's produced coachwork of rather pleasing lines, but I would suggest this was not one of their finest efforts.

On the following page, BMX 331 in even less glamourous times, abandoned at Porton Down!

(J.S. Cockshott Archive; The Transport Library)

It was not until 1947 that the company increased its fleet with the addition of two new vehicles. These were a Leyland Titan PD1 (EAM 776) and a Leyland Tiger PS1/1 (EMW703)

EAM776 seen here in Salisbury (J S Cockshott Archive, The transport Library)

EMW703 seen here in The New Canal Salisbury (Author's collection; unknown)

And at Porton Down at a later date.

(Courtesy Paul Redmond)

EMW703 was to mark an end of an era, as it was the last vehicle delivered in unpainted polished aluminium panelling, which had since its inception been the associated image of Silver Star.

In 1949, three more vehicles were acquired ABN622 Leyland TD5c and two Leyland TD4cs COX966 and COX968

ABN622 a Leyland Titan TD7 a double-decker bought for the Salisbury service, which was already 10 years old, and for which there are few pictures. The only photograph I have seen of this vehicle, in its original specification, is shown below, and strangely for that time, is in colour: this vehicle was withdrawn from public service in 1956 and was converted for use as a tree cutting platform and remained in use in th at guise until 1962.

(Courtesy, The Omnibus Society. Roy Marshall. The transport Library)

The following picture shows ABN662 in use as a hedge cutting platform.

Possibly in the St Marks area of Salisbury or Tidworth (Courtesy Jack Parsons)

And here at Porton, less glamourous. This vehicle was used to collect an aeroplane hangar from Ashford, Kent, which was used to extend the garage at Porton Down.

(Courtesy Jack Parsons)

The next picture shows COX 966 in Blue Boar Row:

And COX 968 at Porton Down Depot: (J.S. Cockshott Archive; The Transport Library)

The next acquisition was in 1951, this was a Leyland PD2/1 GWV360 and is shown below in Blue Boar Row: (Unknown)

During the 1950s, one of Silver Star's main incomes was from weekend leave express coach services for the Forces stationed at local military camps.

Wilts and Dorset had pioneered this type of service from Boscombe Down to London. Many licence applications for this type of service were turned down. But in 1952 Silver Star were operating express services from Bulford, Porton and Winterbourne, and by 1953 they had further licences to operate from Bulford, Tidworth and Perham Down to Birmingham, Manchester and Liverpool. Wilts and Dorset also had similar licences and there was much rivalry which ended up in the Traffic Courts.

Because Silver Star always had a loyal following locally, customers would usually allow a Wilts and Dorset bus to go by, and wait for the preferred "Star" service to arrive.

This type of business of course called for different types of vehicles, and in 1952 Silver star acquired 2 Leyland royal tiger coaches HWV793 and JMR736.

The following picture is a rare colour shot of GWV360 and KGU263 in the depot in Pennyfarthing St. Salisbury.

(courtesy Dave Mant)

JMR736

JMR736 as received by Silver Star, before having roof box added or being sign written.

(Courtesy Jack Parsons)

JMR 736 at Porton Down (Courtesy Paul Redmond)

All the post-war Silver Star coaches had heaters which was by no means standard at that time, and they were also quite luxurious in the seating compared with many of their competitors. Radios too were a must for the troops, and these were state of the art for the time.

During the summers, these coaches would often be hired out to other operators, further increasing the revenue.

The following rare photograph is HWV793 in its original body form, prior to being rebodied following an accident in 1956 (see later). Notice that the circle surrounding the star on the roof box is uniquely white and not as on all the other vehicles, black.

(Courtesy Jack Parsons, from Haines collection)

In 1955 3 more coaches were purchased. These were Leyland PSUC1/2s (KMW643-644 and LMW483)

1956 was an unfortunate year for Silver Star. At 02.40on 30th April, HWV793 crashed into trees at Birdingbury near Rugby, on the return trip from Newcastle, following the servicemen's weekend leave. The crash killed 5 servicemen that day and one later in hospital and injured ca 20 others. The crash was believed to be caused by a suitcase, or possibly a metal first aid box falling from the luggage rack onto the driver's head causing him to fall from his seat and lose control of the vehicle. After seeing the driver fall, it was reported that one passenger got hold of the steering wheel and tried to gain control. The driver was Reg Bowley of lower Bemerton, Salisbury. In a following inquest into the accident, the jury returned verdicts of Accidental deaths and suggested that no rack for the accommodation of moveable objects should be constructed above the driver's head on public service vehicles. I am told that there was some suggestion that high-jinks had been the cause of the accident and that one of the passengers was driving or attempting to, although no evidence of that emerged.

HWV793 accident in April 1956. A police spokesman said that the bus was all but cut in two.

It says something of the resilience of Silver Star, and of the somewhat austere times, that this vehicle was rebuilt with a new body, in some reports as soon as July of that year.

The following picture is said to be of the Harrington body plate for HWV793

(Courtesy Martin Perry)

HMV793 as rebodied to C41C style after an accident in 1956 (Courtesy Paul Redmond)

KMW 643 in Leeds (Courtesy The Transport Library)

KMW644 Possibly at Tidworth? (Author's collection, unknown)

LMW483 in Leeds (Courtesy J S Cockshott Archive; The Transport Library)

The coaching service was an excellent revenue for Silver Star, but the company did not neglect its local trade.

So, during that year came GKL 763, another Leyland TD7, which is shown outside the Cadena Café in the Blue Boar Row, Salisbury.

(LTHL Collection), and in the following, less flattering rear-view in the wash-bay at Porton Down.

(Courtesy J S Cockshott Archive; The transport Library)

Another 3 coaches were also to make their first appearance in 1956; two Leyland PSUC1/2s (MMR 552-553) and a Commer Contender IV (NMW340)

MMR552 seen here in Leeds (Courtesy J S Cockshott; The Transport Library)

This picture taken on 26th march 1961 shows the earlier Silver Star device on the side flash. Note also there are no wheel trims. I am told by Jack Parsons that there were never enough wheels trims for all the vehicles and that they were routinely swapped between vehicles.

In a photograph of August 1961, the device has been changed to "Silver Star Services" as in the following picture:

(Courtesy Jack Parsons)

And MMR 553 also in Leeds. Note variation in paintwork and Silver Star logo between MMR 552 and MMR 553 (Courtesy J S Cockshott Archive; The Transport Library)

Commer Contender IV NMW 340 (Author's collection: from Gillard)

In 1957 Silver Star applied for another express licence from Porton Down to the newly built Bemerton Heath housing project so that workers at Porton would not have to break their journey in Salisbury, and despite much objection from the competition, (Wilts & Dorset and British Rail) this licence was granted.

To accommodate this the company purchased in that year, one of what was to be the first of a small fleet of one-man operated vehicles. The first of these was PHR 829, a Leyland PSUC1/2, as seen in the following pictures:

Photo © John Kaye. Please do not re-post without permission.

My thanks to David Lang and John Boylett of www.sct61.org.co,uk for permission to use this picture.

Also, in 1957 Silver Star purchased OHR280 and 281, two Harrington bodied Leyland PSU1/2s which were converted from central to front entry bodies in 1962: There seem to be more pictures of these two buses post-Silver Star, than with the company. The following two pictures show OHR 280 in Silver Star colours and OHR281 in Silver Star livery but just after the W&D takeover, and with the Silver Star logo painted out:

(Courtesy Dave Mant)

This was followed by three more PSUC1/2s in 1958. (PMW386, RAM 620 and SAM 47

These are the buses with which I, and I suspect other contemporary locals are probably most familiar, and I wonder how many hours I have spent on them, especially the last bus back to Porton at night?

(Author collection; unknown)

PMW 386 shown in the previous photo, a picture which has always been one of my favourites. It looks like at least three Silver Star buses on a trip to the seaside. The picture is probably posed to capture the child jumping for joy at being at the seaside but nevertheless captures the moment and stimulates a nostalgia for those times.

RAM 620, a similar-looking addition to the fleet is seen here outside the Cadena Café in Blue Boar Row. Salisbury

(Author collection: unknown)

And SAM 47, still in Silver Star Livery but with the logo painted out on 20th June 1963, just a few days after the W&D takeover.

(Courtesy Dave Mant)

This coach together with OHR 280 and OHR 281 had some very special body detailing, in the form of a dorsal fin as seen in the following picture;

(Courtesy Dave Mant)

Was there any reason for these Art Deco streamlining fins? The answer is of course no except that the designers were following the creations coming out of Detroit, where every car of that period sported such fins and jet nozzles, and this was only because one of the designers had been in aviation prior to that. Harrington first used this type of device as early as 1935 but these were applied to the roof only, not bisecting the rear windows as in the examples shown on the Silver Star coaches. But even in the 1950s, these were futuristic machines for what had once been a very rural bus company. These later finned vehicles had outlet vents in the fins, which expelled cigarette smoke via an extractor fan.

1959 was a very special year for Silver Star, and a very memorable one for boys of my age, in that they were the very first independent company to deploy the Leyland Atlantean DR1/1 (TMW 853). This model bus seemed to be way ahead of its time, and in the somewhat austere times in which other bus companies were still using buses from the 1930s and

1940s, Silver Star was also ahead of the game. To a ten-year-old boy, these vehicles seemed like spaceships compared with the others in the fleet and it was of great concern to be the first to ride in one and that I do remember very well.

With the engine at the back and its sheer front, I think these buses would still not look out of place in a modern fleet, and that Silver Star was courageous enough to order these in those uncertain times, makes them very special.

The fabulous new Silver Star Atlantean in Blue Boar Row Salisbury. A very early picture prior to any advertisements. The hardware store Pinder's later had its name on that side of the bus, and P. Nicholl's piano specialists of Queen St. on the other.

Just to put things into perspective, the next purchase made by the company was a 1949 Leyland 7RT (KGU 263) which came from London Transport.

It seems a bit of a contradiction that the company was buying 10-year-old high mileage vehicles like this when they were so far ahead of their time with the Atlanteans, but I am sure there were good business reasons for this.

KGU 263 at Porton Down (Courtesy The transport Library

The second Atlantean also arrived that year and that was VAM 944:

Atlantean VAM 944 (Author collection; D. Gillard)

In 1960 the company purchased two Leyland L1s (WAM 441 and WWV 564)

WWV 564 Salisbury (Author collection; D. Gillard)

WAM 441 at Porton Down (Courtesy Peter Gould)

The next photograph is of a rare glimpse into the Harrington works, where a Silver Star vehicle is being constructed, with the panelling around the roof box taking shape. I have included this picture here because it is thought that this was WAM 441 being b uilt, this seems to be borne out by the Harrington list.

(Courtesy Jack Parsons)

1961 saw the introduction of another Atlantean (XMW 706) as shown below:

Atlantean XMW 706 (Author's collection, Unknown)

The coach interior of XMW706 (courtesy Jack Parsons)

And also, in that year a novel addition in the form of a 13 seat Trojan minibus.

Trojan 367 BAA (Courtesy Martin Coull)

And with Atlantean VAM 944 (Courtesy LTHL Collection)

I don't think I remember this rather charming little vehicle. It was Silver Star's penultimate acquisition and was also the last vehicle to operate under Silver Star ownership. It was Christened Baa Baa for obvious reasons and the nickname appears on the front panel.

The last vehicle purchased by Silver Star was Leyland Atlantean (1013MW) and will be familiar to even those locals who have no recollections of Silver Star, as being the beautifully restored example that regularly appears at old bus gatherings and has more than once done memorial tours around its old routes around Porton.

Finally, in 1962 the last bus purchased was Atlantean 1013 MW.

Atlantean 1013MW seen here on an excursion to the seaside. (Unknown)

Yet one more vehicle which seems to have escaped previous commentators is the one shown in the next photograph, and again I do not remember ever seeing this one. There seems to be no information on when this vehicle was purchased, except that this appears to be the Morris variant, and so could have been purchased between 1959 and 1963. With its liking for innovative vehicles, it is just possible Silver Star purchased this van in the earlier stages of production (1960), but not known for sure.

(Unknown)

XAM 918, A delightful Minivan service vehicle, on which the company has gone to great lengths to promote the corporate image, with the addition of the Top Box incorporating the familiar logo. Note also the red flash to the side of the van and the silver star on the radiator grille.

Further information on this vehicle comes from Jack Parsons, who tells me it was driven by his uncle Don Parsons on his inspector duties. The van was not in fact silver as might be suggested from the photograph, but remained in its original colour of Nevada Beige. That Silver Star should go to all that trouble of presenting the vehicle in the corporate image but not bother to change the body colour to silver seems atypical of the company's philosophy. Did they know its life with the firm would be short?

There was also a Bedford lorry 5612MV included in the fleet.

The demise of Silver Star.

Two main factors seem to be responsible for the demise of the Silver Star company; firstly, the express trade from Salisbury plain to the North, mainly troops travelling on weekend leave had started to decline and the refusal of the Traffic Commissioners to allow the use of Atlanteans on these routes, despite several applications from Silver Star, only exacerbated the situation.

Secondly, was the death of founder Eddie Shergold, who by all accounts had always been the driving force behind the company. Even before this loss, the other partner Ben White had let it be known that he wished to retire. Shergold's death, therefore, was the catalyst that was to drive in the final nail and precipitate the end of a company that was gradually becoming less viable.

So, at midnight on June 4th, 1963 Silver Star was taken over by its old adversary Wilts & Dorset. The transition which was advertised as a "merger" was in name only, and Wilts and Dorset were somewhat overzealous in their haste to obliterate all traces of the Silver Star name, sending in the painters to overwrite the Silver Star logos on the buses, even before the agreed time of takeover. One of these, sent from W&D to paint over the silver star logos, was Morris Englebretson.

The following picture taken a few days before the takeover, shows RAM620 at the Wilts and Dorset depot. Apparently, it was involved in an accident when a car crashed into the back of it, as driver Pat James was stopped to let passengers off in Porton Village. The bus was repaired by Locomotors of Andover and ended up at the W&D depot, where it was repainted.

Peter Gould's brief account of Silver Star's history, tells us that on the 4th of June 1963 at about 11 pm the last Silver Star (Trojan 367 BAA) vehicle pulled into the depot at Porton Down and so ended the days of Silver Star Motor Services.

The following pictures were taken shortly before closure. The proud line-up of Atlanteans is very evocative of the times, I think. The last vehicle on the right is No.18 GWV360 as far as I can make out, and is in the internal shed photo.

(Courtesy Mike Sutcliffe MBE)

(Courtesy Mike Sutcliffe MBE)

So, a very sad day for the company, the loyal staff and the very loyal local customers.

Although the express trade was diminishing, the business was still viable in 1963 and had the death of Eddie Shergold and the retirement of Ben White not occurred at that time, it is possible the business would have continued for many years. As an indicator of the success of the business, Probate lists the E Shergold estate as being £19264 9s. this would amount to ca £400,000 today (2021). Not a vast sum, but suggesting a degree of solvency.

What happened next?

A look at the fate of some of the Silver Star fleet

So of course, staff were made redundant, and some went on to work for Wilts and Dorset and some drivers carrying on driving the very same buses, but in a different paint scheme.

Although most of the Silver Star fleet was absorbed into the Wilts and Dorset fleet, some vehicles never saw service with the new owners and were very quickly sold on to other companies.

It is difficult to understand exactly the choices Wilts and Dorset made, regarding which vehicles to keep and which to sell on, but there remains some history of most of the vehicles absorbed from Silver Star. The fact that in most cases, the very characteristic destination boards and illuminated logo signs were not removed but painted over means it is quite easy even for a non-expert like me to spot them immediately in any livery.

I have endeavoured here to show the fate of some of the ex- Silver Star fleet, which I think has not been adequately attempted before. It is by no means a complete account but will give the reader an insight into the destiny of at least some of the fleet. It is a mostly depressing description, especially those shown in abandonment, but also in some cases heartening to see how some of these vehicles have been brought back from dying hulks to shining examples of the company's fleet. Where possible, I have tried to show the ex-Silver Star vehicles in colour so as to contrast the different liveries of the new owners.

Occasionally the new livery did justice to the vehicles, but mostly what we see is a quick lick of paint and the buses remain obviously "ex-Silver Star" to any enthusiast. We have seen before how Wilts & Dorset were somewhat overzealous in their race to remove all traces of their long-term adversaries, but after a time even they presented these buses in a reasonably smart way.

HWV793

HWV793 saw service with W&D and is seen in the following picture at the depot in Castle Street, Salisbury in March 1967

(Courtesy Dave Mant)

The next picture shows HWV793 with Berresfords, at PMT in Hanley. It is thought it was withdrawn around 1971. It was at Ripley's (bus dealer), Carlton, South Yorkshire in May 1987

JMR736

JMR736 was not used by W&D, but was sold on to Western National, in whose livery it is seen in the following picture:

(Courtesy David Lang)

And at a later date was used by a company called Goullee of Bexhill Road, London, as in the following photo:

(Courtesy Barry Nunn)

KMW643 and 644

These two Leyland, Harrington bodied coaches both saw service with Western National:

KMW643 in Western National colours (Courtesy Chris Stanley)

And KMW644

(Courtesy Brian Bennett)

KMW644, (and 643) were with Jolly Bus of South Hylton, Sunderland:

KMW644 with Jolly at Teesside Oil refinery July 1967 (J S Cockshott's Archive; The Transport Library)

LMW483

The Leyland Burlingham LMW483 saw service with Western National following the W&D takeover of Silver Star. It is seen here in Plymouth circa the mid-1960s:

(Courtesy Barney Staples)

The Silver Star roof box looks a little incongruous on the flowing lines of this vehicle.

LMW483 was then used by Jolly of South Hylton, Sunderland, and is seen in the following picture at Teesside Oil Refinery in July 1967:

And in the following picture, in North's Dealership and scrapyard at Sherburn in Elmet also in 1967:

And that seems to be the last we hear of LMW483

(Courtesy J S Cockshott; the Transport Library)

NMW340

This only non-Leyland coach operated by Silver Star, post-war, Commer Contender NMW340 did not see service with Wilts and Dorset, but was purchased by Western National, under royal Blue livery:

(Courtesy, The Ken Steley collection)

And here in the following picture at Southend, in service with Elms Coaches of Kenton, Middlesex:

(Courtesy Mike Walker)

And at a later date, approaching extinction In Elms yard:

(Courtesy Chris Stanley; B Maguire collection)

PHR829

PHR829 served with W&D for some years and is seen in the following picture, in Salisbury in April of 1967. (Courtesy Dave Mant):

RAM 620 in Red and Cream W&D livery, seen here in March 1967 in Salisbury Bus Station. Subsequently, the vehicle was painted red to the whole body. Apparently, this bus ended up at a company called Blackwell Hodge in Randalstown, Northern Ireland and was there in 1979 and then later scrapped.

(Courtesy Dave Mant)

PMW386

PMW386 saw several years' service with Wilts and Dorset

PMW 386 in W&D colours in February 1968

(Courtesy Dave Mant)

In later life, it was with Pioneer coaches of Laugharne, South Carmarthenshire.

Note that the photographer has changed the destination board to Allington. It appears that the vehicle has been withdrawn from service at this time?

Most of the vehicles although painted, would, because of the iconic roof boxes still be instantly recognizable as ex-Silver Star fleet, especially to the local customers.

The next picture shows WWV 564 looking resplendent in W&D cream and red paintwork in April 1968

(Courtesy Dave Mant)

And in different colours but with the same company in July 1972 (Courtesy Dave Mant)

This vehicle seems to have ended its life with Eynon's of Trimsaran, Carmarthenshire Where it is seen in the following photograph, in the company's yard in the late1970s:

(Courtesy John Law)

OHR280-281

The chronology of these two coaches is less clear than with other ex-silver Star vehicles: The picture below shows either OHR280 or 281 (probably 281 because of the ariel?) in Keswick in the early 1960s in Wilts and Dorset livery:

(Photo by Frank Walton)

(Courtesy Dave Mant)

In the picture above, OHR 280 on the far right is seen in Charlies Cars of Bournemouth livery, and is on loan to wilts and Dorset, whilst OHR 281, at the rear is in Shamrock and Rambler livery and is also on loan to W&D. Salisbury, March 1967. Later they were in the hands of Berresford's, 280 is shown in their livery in July 1970 in Longton:

(Courtesy Nick Blurton)

By 1976, both OHR 280 and 281 have been consigned to the Berresford scrap heap, where they are seen in the following picture in May 1976:

(Courtesy Michael Barbour)

And looking depressingly forlorn in July 1977

(Courtesy Dave Mant)

SAM47

The following picture shows SAM47 just after the W&D takeover, still in Silver Star livery, but with the name and logo whitewashed out.

In Salisbury, 20th June 1963 (Courtesy Dave Mant)

And in Wilts and Dorset livery at Salisbury, February 1970. Courtesy (Dave Mant)

There seems to be little more information on this vehicle, except in the following picture it is shown with a "delicenced" notice on the windscreen, and the Wilts and Dorset Roofbox name blank. October 1971. Courtesy Dave Mant):

MMR552

MMR 552 went to W&D but was not used by the company, and its first reincarnation was with Western National as part of the Royal Blue fleet.

Here is MMR552 see here in its Royal Blue (Western National) colours

(Courtesy J S Cockshott Archive' The Transport Library)

In 1967 the vehicle was in the hands of Webbers at Blisland. Nr Bodmin

MMR552 at Webber's of Blisland, Bodmin July 1972

in 1972 it was acquired by Whiteheads of Cheltenham.

MMR552 at Whiteheads of Cheltenham; (Flashes Coaches).

It was then acquired by dealer Martin Perry, and by mid-1977 it belonged to Simon Turner of Bath with a view to restoration.

In the following picture, MMR552 is seen arriving at Highbury Engineering, between Mells and Coleford, where it was stored for ca 2 years. After this time, it was again towed to Bruton where it resided for the next 4 years or so.

And here, languishing in the yard of the Brutonian Bus Company in June 1978:

(Courtesy Dave Mant)

In the early 1980s, it was noticed by Ron Hayter, who made Jack Parsons aware of it. Jack acquired it in 1984

And on the previous page, at Barton Park, Eastleigh in October 1984, and belonging to Jack Parsons where it appears to be partly restored in etch primer or undercoat, but there was no engine in it at the time.

Restored to Silver Star specification in the Red Lion premises (at that time owned by Ron Hayter) at Eastleigh.

In 2007 it was owned by Geoff and Ian Norris.

MMR553

MMR 553 like its sister was not used by Wilts and Dorset but was used initially as part of the western National Royal blue fleet.

MMR553 in Royal Blue livery, seen here in Exeter, July 1966. (Courtesy Brian Bennett)

And here in July 1969 being used by Friends of Disabled on a trip to Falmouth. Until I came across this picture during research for this book, I had never seen reference to this vehicle being in the hands of this group:

MMR553 with Friends of Disabled (Courtesy of Chris Stanton)

In the 1970s, the vehicle was owned by Deeble of Upton Cross near Liskeard. MMR553 operated for some years, from outside the Liskeard railway Station:

MMR553 in Deeble livery (Courtesy Ian Trotter)

MMR553 looking slightly less glamourous in Deeble's Yard, with ex-Silver Star Atlantean VAM944 behind:

It was acquired by David Dawes in 1980 for restoration.

KGU263 Leyland RTL ex London Transport

This bus had a very varied life. From London Transport, it was sold to Birds Commercial Motors of Stratford-upon-Avon, from where Silver Star bought it in September 1959. Post Silver Star, it went to Super coaches of Upminster in June 1963 and then it was used in the Matchbox Lesney Staff Transport Fleet.

There seem to be no pictures of it whilst at Lesney. It was bought by S Ledgard in March 1965 where it served for two years and is seen in that guise in the following picture:

It then went to Canvey Island and from there to Wickford Coaches but was not used. It was then bought for restoration by Ted Bracknell and Terry Robertson and painted back to LT red. In 1970 it was displayed in Brighton and Stratford-upon-Avon:

KGU 263 at Brighton May 1970, in London Transport livery, following restoration. Sadly, this bus was destroyed by fire in June of 1970.

(Courtesy Dave Mant)

I am told on good authority that the engine to this vehicle does survive in a barn somewhere in South Devon.

VAM 944

This vehicle seems to have had the most colourful history of all the ex-Silver Star fleet.

After the closure of Silver Star, this bus passed via Wilts and Dorset to Bristol Omnibus, where it became N0.7998 based at Weston-Super-Mare:

In September of 1964 it was acquired by Super Coaches of Upminster:

(J S Cockshott Archive, The Transport library)

It was then sold on to Berresford Motors, Cheddleton and then onwards to Hale-Trent Cakes Ltd. of Clevedon:

(Courtesy Neil Jennings)

Just after the above picture was taken it was sold on to a Rev. Green, and later operated by Deeble of Upton Cross Cornwall:

Taken from the cover of "Looking back at Independent Double-Deckers" by Andrew Wiltshire.

And here apparently waiting for the end, in Deeble's yard, with its ex-Silver Star stablemate MMR 553:

(Courtesy Of KDH Archives; The Late Keith Holt)

Like VAM 944, Atlanteans XMW 706 and 1013MW progressed to Berresford Motors after having been in the hands of Super Coaches for a while.

Rare colour picture XMW706 in Super Coaches livery, taken in Long Metford, Suffolk. May 1966... (Courtesy Brian Bennett.)

The roof box remains intact, with the Super Coaches name on the front and rear name boards.

I am not sure if it has been abandoned in the previous photo, or just broken down, the former I would think. And with Berresford's at a later date.

Although in monochrome it would appear that the paintwork has not been changed from Silver Star's days, but the main colour is cream rather than Silver. (Courtesy of Len Wright Images)

Very sadly, this lovely vehicle ended its days languishing in Berresford's yard and was totally wrecked by fire, as seen in the following very sad picture:

(Courtesy of Bryan Bareham)

Atlantean 1013MW (also going to Super Coaches and then Berresford's) had an altogether different fate, although its journey to that end was similar to the others:

It first appears in splendid Bristol Omnibus green, and having had the Silver Star roof-box removed before being sold on:

(Courtesy Geoff Pullin) July 1963. 1013MW with Bristol Omnibus Company. I am told that the Bristol Company even changed the steering wheel to a white colour, to indicate to the driver that the vehicle was over 7' 6" in width.

Courtesy of Geoff Pullin).

If this date is correct, and there is no reason to dispute this, then Bristol wasted no time in getting the vehicle into their own colours. Considering that on 4th June 1963, the bus was still in Silver Star livery, and only went to Wilts and Dorset on the 6th June, it seems that Bristol did a very quick but pleasing transformation.

I think Bristol Omnibus were the only firm to really do justice to the ex-Silver Star vehicles, (although some of the later Wilts & Dorset examples did look smart).Certainly, Bristol was the only company to take the trouble to remove the Silver Star roof boxes. According to Geoff Pullin, this picture was taken probably on the first day of service with Bristol Omnibus, (July 1963) it certainly looks very shiny.

The following picture shows 1013MW, still presumably in its Bristol livery. It appears to have taken quite a knock to the front near side. The destination board reads "PRIVATE Upminster & District"

Note that much of the chrome trim has been removed (possibly as a result of the front damage?) Also, I note that the white steering wheel has worn away in places to the original black. (Courtesy Len Wright)

And on the previous page, still with super coaches, but on hire to London Transport. Note the damage above the rear wheel, typically caused by a tyre blowout I am told.

(Courtesy Stuart Johnson)

And in the following; a not so aesthetically pleasing livery with Berresford's in September 1976. Note that some, but not all of the chrome trim has been replaced to the front and sides of the vehicle, although the lower front offside piece appears to be hanging off.

(Courtesy of Nick Blurton)

And this lovely shot from July 1977:

(Courtesy Dave Mant)

I am told that we are to be very thankful to Berresford's, in that they were always very reluctant to dispose of their vehicles which became obsolete or surplus to requirements, and this was one of the factors which resulted in this vehicle being saved. (see restoration section).

In the following pictures it is seen lying in the Berresford yard, gradually disintegrating, but extant

(Unknown)

(Courtesy Richard Morant; The Transport Library)

TMW 853

Atlantean TMW 853 went also to Bristol Omnibus and then to Super Coaches, but was then purchased by Midas Motor Services of Brentwood in1966. There is some mystery attached to this vehicle as discussed below. There is one account that suggests it ended up in America, but I have no more on that.

Here it is in Bristol Omnibus Livery (Courtesy Geoff Pullen): Note White steering wheel as per 1013MW whilst at Bristol. (Courtesy Mike Walker)

TMW853 with Midas but on hire to Southend Corporation during the 1967 strike. The strike started as an overtime ban on 3rd November. The management quickly drafted in buses and crews from other companies, mostly from Super Coaches of Upminster, but as the a bove photo shows, also from Midas of Brentwood. Because of this use of other firms, the strike escalated to full stoppage and lasted for some 5 weeks. A mystery here is why the bus is painted red. One commentator on this photograph on a popular website stated it was still in its Bristol Omnibus livery but of course, that company's livery was Tilling Green, and Midas in its short history tended to use silver and blue livery, as in the picture of the same vehicle, still with the firm in 1969 shows. From Bristol Omnibus, it seems that the vehicle was purchased by PVS (Passenger Vehicle Sales which traded in second-hand stock from the same premises as Super Coaches. Much of this stock went to "or was lent" to Super Coaches. Some of the stock going to the USA. PVS later moved to Silver End in Essex

The next picture is said to be whilst at Midas Motor Services of Brentwood in 1969, but looks more like Super coaches' livery?

(unknown)

Note there is no logo on the side of the bus? Midas ceased trading in the early 1970s, and as one commentator put it TMW “seemed to fall off the face of the earth”, so the suggestion that it went to America seems more credible, although the trail certainly goes cold at this time and I can find no trace of it in the USA.

367 BAA

This interesting little vehicle was purchased by silver Star in 1961. Although it went to Wilts & Dorset, it wasn’t used by them but was repainted a cream colour by them.

Post Silver Star it was used in Bath to ferry tourists between the Pump Room and the Assembly Rooms. In the following picture, it is seen in a cream-coloured livery.

367BAA in its W&D cream colour, on duty in Bath. (J S Cockshott Archive; The Transport Library)

In 1967 it was painted in a two-tone colour scheme by the same company:

It was sold on in 1970.

(Courtesy Mike Walker)

THE SILVER STAR STAFF

An early photograph of proprietors Ben White and Eddie Shergold (in bow tie):

It seems that Silver Star had a really good relationship with their staff. The ex-members of staff or relations of ex-staff I have spoken to, all regard their time there as special. The number of reunions of the staff with each other and with the restored vehicles stands testament to the regard with which the company was held. These members of staff, all kept mementoes of their time with the company and were proud to show them off. The Silver Star lapel badge, seems to be a very treasured item, but others have kept their driver/conductor number badges as well, and one conductress even had her Silver Star jacket complete with monogram silver buttons.

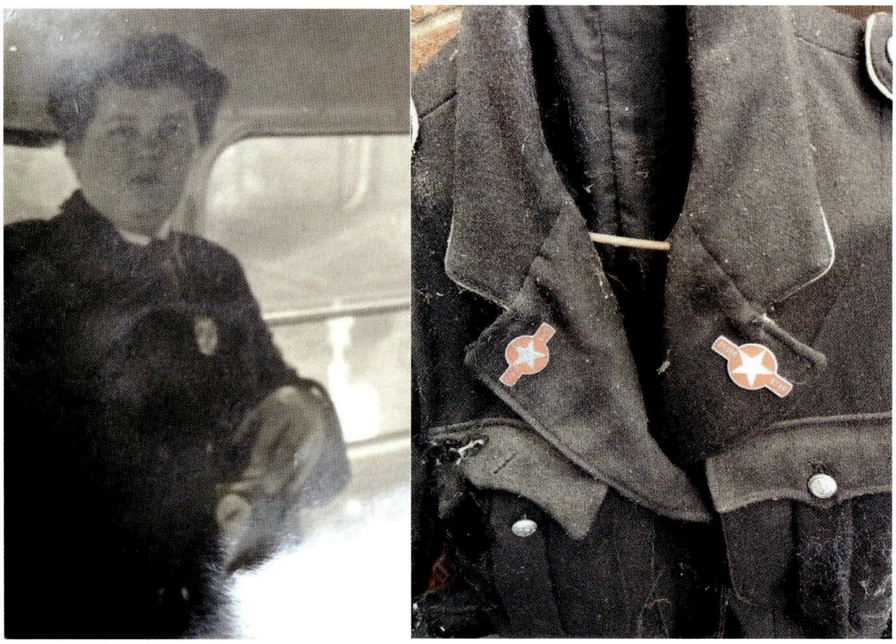

Naomi Jean Laidlaw (nee Benham) And the jacket she saved for more than 60 years.

The hardware from the jacket. (Courtesy Naomi Jean Laidlaw)

From Mary Dixon

Brian Thorne, Jill Thorne, Dougie Tillier? And Ted White

(Courtesy Naomi Jean Laidlaw)

And these two rather wonderful pictures above of Peggy and Reg Snelgrove, posing very proudly in their Silver Star uniforms. Peggy was a conductress and Reg a driver. (Courtesy Di Snelgrove)

Joan Shergold, Yvonne White and Greta Tanswell, looking extremely smart in their express hostess uniforms.

(Courtesy Jack Parsons)

(Courtesy Jack Parsons)

Silver Star Staff (ca 1961-62)

From left; Ray Todd, Dave Coleman, George Hudson, Dave Ashburner, Bill Coleman (in white shirt). Staff inside garage unknown. On the right Mary Dixon (nee Porter) (Information and photo courtesy Jack Parsons).

(Courtesy Jack Parsons)

This fabulous photograph was taken of the staff on the day of closure, and I am indebted to Jack Parsons for allowing me to use it.

Seen here, from left to right, looking perhaps happier than they were:

Ben White, Greta Tanswell, Ron Mowland, Doug, Tillier, Ron Parsons, Stan Coleman, Jock Lennon (with glasses), Gordon White, A 16-year-old Jack Parsons, Ken Hartley, Bill Coleman (in white), George Hudson, Dave Coleman, Reg Todd, Percy Newman, Roy Brewer, Yvonne White and Bill Ashburner.

Bill Webb took the photograph.

Also, on that day, a reporter and photographer were sent out from the Salisbury Journal to cover the closure. Apparently, they were arrested by the MoD Police, for use of a camera on MoD property, and the film was confiscated.

Driver Don Parsons with Eddie Shergold's Bentley (Courtesy Jack Parsons)

We do not know who the inspector is, but a fantastic picture of the Silver Star bus stop at Policeman's Corner, Winterbourne Gunner. The wording within the star is "BUS PASSENGERS & INSPECTOR".

(Courtesy Bourne Valley History Society)

Both Ben White and Eddie Shergold had something other than Silver Star in common, in their liking of unusual gates to the entrances to their respective properties. Eddies property, "Brooklands" at Winterbourne Gunner sported elaborate double gates to the entrance, decorated by two golden lions. What the significance of the lions was, and why silver stars were not chosen is unknown. All of the people local to Winterbourne Gunner that I have spoken to, remember these gates well as they were really quite grand and imposing. Strangely, there seem to be no photographs of these landmarks. There is however a picture of the pedestrian gate to the property which bore the motto "Wha Daur Meddle Wi' Me".

This strange expression which is on the royal coat of arms of Scotland and was also the motto of the Black Watch Regiment originates from the Latin “Nemo me impune lacessit”, which in English translates to “Nobody interferes with me with impunity”. The motto on the gate is the broad Scots dialect version.

I have been told that both sets of gates were manufactured in the MoD workshops at Porton Down.

Pedestrian gate to “Brooklands”, Winterbourne Gunner”

(Courtesy Bourne Valley history Society)

In contrast to these splendid but somewhat ostentatious constructions, were the gates which adorned Ben White’s property in Allington. These were apparently fabricated in the Silver Star Garage from scrap iron and some wheel rims which were lying around at the time. Perhaps there is a little irony here, it that whilst the flamboyant gates of Eddie Shergold’s property have long since disappeared, the more frugal examples of Ben Whites property survive to this day:

It is worth noting that even the hinges of these gates are very cleverly constructed from old vehicle track rod ends.

This may also be an appropriate place to show another rustic Silver Star item, which has survived thanks to Jack Parsons. This "OFFICE" sign decorated the external entrance to the office block at Porton Down. It can be seen in situ in the photograph of the forecourt at Porton, with KGU263 shown previously in this book.

(Courtesy Jack Parsons)

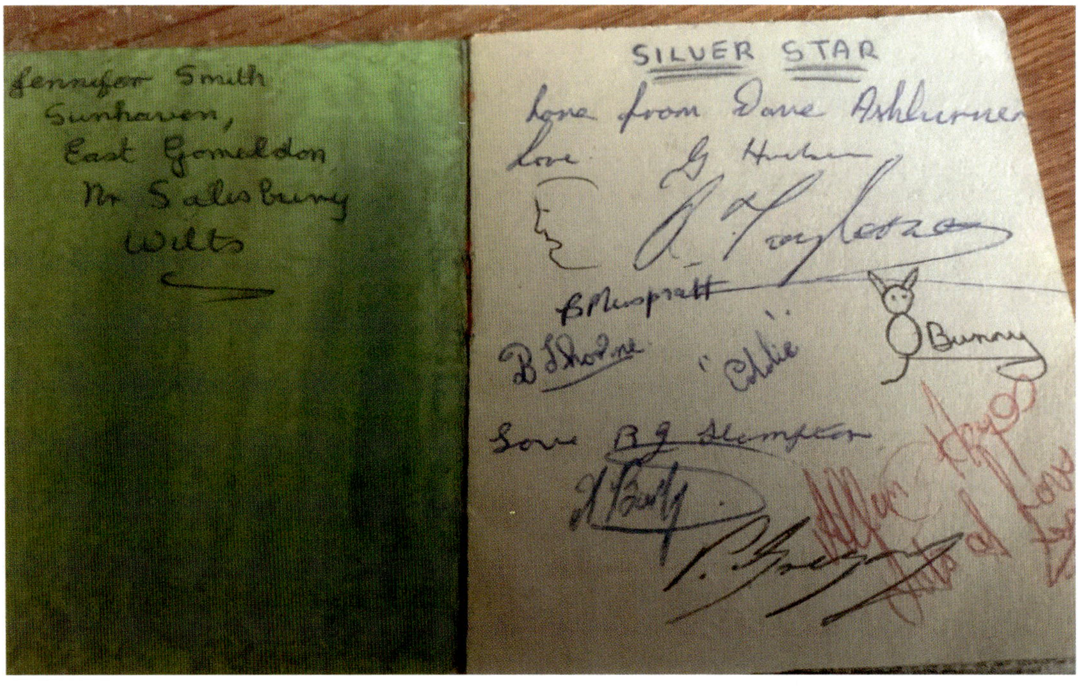

Autograph book with a page of Silver Star staff members, collected by Jennifer Smith

(Courtesy Jack Parsons)

SILVER STAR VEHICLES IN THE BOURNE VALLEY

In this chapter, especially for Bourne Valley locals and ex-locals, and because there are some quality photographs that deserve to be shown, I have included some shots of Silver Star buses on location in and around Porton, Idmiston, Allington and Gomeldon.

Photograph was given by Mary Dixon (unknown)

And all three restored vehicles, outside the Porton Memorial Hall:

(Courtesy Dave Mant)

IDMISTON

VAM944 at Idmiston. (Unknown)

And 1013MW at the same location in the early 1960s:

(Unknown)

MMR553 on the same bridge in Idmiston as the previous two pictures. (Courtesy Dave Mant)

ALLINGTON

MMR553 at Allington, with Silver Star bus stop sign. (Courtesy Dave Mant)

MMR552 at Allington, with the most loyal of ex -Silver Star staff member Mary Dixon

(Photo given by Mary Dixon)

1013MW and MMR552 at The Old Inn Allington.

(Photo given by Mary Dixon)

GOMELDON

1013MW at Gomeldon triangle, (Courtesy Dave Mant)

RAM620 in W&D livery at Gomeldon triangle June 1969 (Courtesy Dave Mant)

WWV564 at Gomeldon Triangle June 1971(Courtesy Dave Mant)

WAM441 in W&D livery June 1970 (Courtesy Dave Mant)

WINTERBOURNE

MMR553 in Winterbourne May 1982 (Courtesy Dave Mant)

The three restored vehicles, not actually in the Bourne Valley, but near the old forces route at Rollestone Camp, and included as it is the best picture I have seen of this group.

(Courtesy Dave Mant)

SILVER STAR GARAGE

In the little that has been written about Silver Star in the near 100 years since its inception, nothing it seems has been penned about the garage or depot. Bearing in mind that the base for Silver Star was unique, in that during its existence it was within a chemical warfare/ defence research establishment, and surrounded by 7000 acres of War Office/ MoD ranges, I find it strange that this has been overlooked.

In the photograph of the Silver Star fleet in 1927 (seen earlier in this book), the buses are depicted in front of the garage. As described earlier it is possible to determine the width of that garage by counting the corrugations on the cladding, and this is 25 ft.

In the section of a 1917 map of the site seen below, there is a store (shown in red), which from the scale of the map is 9 metres in width which is equivalent to 25ft:

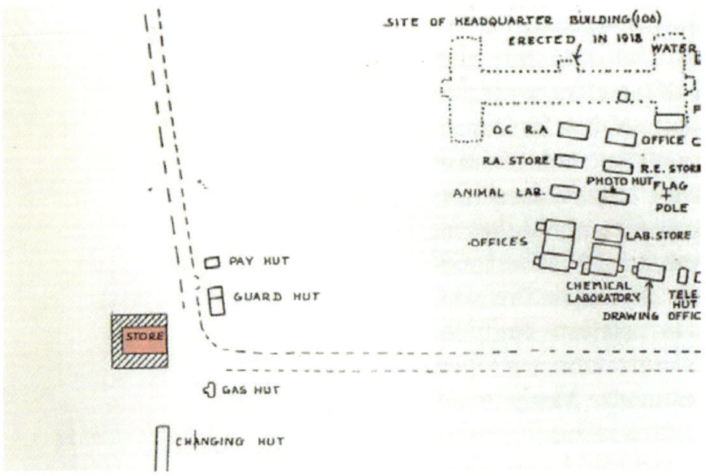

Note how close this building is to the chemical laboratory, although these buildings were resituated after the headquarters building was erected in 1918, but were still in place in 1922. The shaded area around the store represents the site of a pre-1916 building.

Since we know that this is the approximate site of the first Silver Star garage at Porton Camp, it is not I think unreasonable to suggest that it was this building that was taken over by Shergold and White, sometime before 1927.

How the two proprietors managed to acquire this site and building and under what conditions is not known. It was the only commercial premises allowed on the whole of the vast WD establishment. Presumably, the title was on a lease, but I would think there would have been conditions that it could be revoked should the need arise? With their military backgrounds, I suppose it is possible they knew people of influence in the Camp at that time?

The store is shown on a map of 1922 but is missing in 1939 and a building of similar proportions is shown about 60 metres south-west of the original store site:

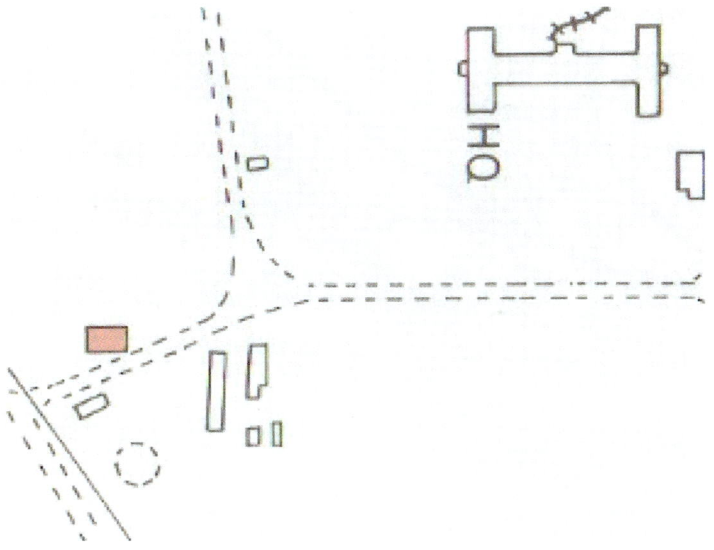

From a map of 1939. Note that laboratories in front of the HQ building have been removed. The line adjacent to the track at the lower left is the Porton Camp Light Railway. On several maps, the area around this building and to the north is marked as allotment gardens. Although the building is not marked as the Silver Star garage, the following aerial photograph of that time (just at the start of WW2) shows a building in that position being used by Silver Star and with the allotment clearly visible: This building (shown in red on the above map and in the aerial photograph), appears to be somewhat smaller than that seen on the 1952 map of the same location, so was perhaps an intermediate building?

Aerial photograph of the Silver Star bus depot ca 1939

Although not shown on the 1939 map, the photograph shows a building on the site of the original War Office store, (near the T junction). Is this the same building, or perhaps part of the allotments? On a later map (1952) this is shown as being the Silver Star Office.

The following photograph shows a new garage being erected:

(Courtesy Jack Parsons)

The building we see in the aerial photograph, is not in quite the same location, and appears smaller than that on the 1952 map? So, the above picture of the building being erected was therefore after 1939 but probably before 1945, since TR5945 is shown before being chopped and converted to a lorry which it has been suggested was ca 1945. It appears to be the main (i.e., front building), which was in situ until closure in 1963. The roof trusses are the same as those seen in later pictures of the interior of that building and the number of bays is the same. In the picture, there is a rope going from the back of the bus up and over one of the truss members, and it may be they are using the bus to raise some of the component parts?

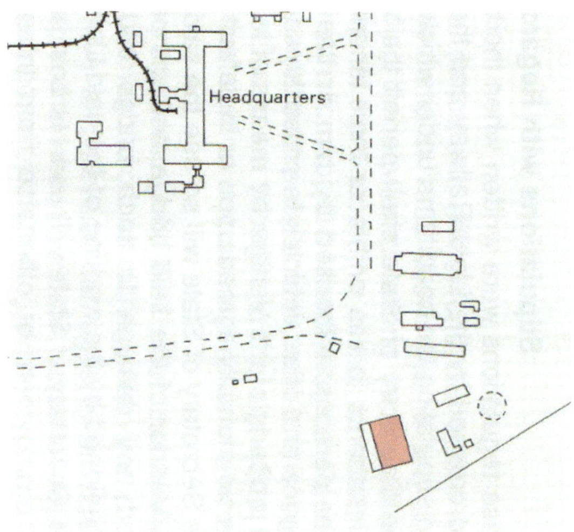

Map of 1952 showing the Silver Star garage in red with the adjacent office addition in white.

(Courtesy Jack Parsons)

The picture above is fascinating, in that it shows the re-erection of an aeroplane hangar, which was used to extend the existing facilities, and was positioned at 90 degrees to that garage. It is not known why the extension was built at right angles to the existing, perhaps because there was not enough land to accommodate the hangar if it was 175ft long? Not visible here but when enlarged, it is just possible to make out what is probably the lines of the Light Railway running through the hangar, as I am told it did. This may infer that the picture is actually a little later, say 1954, after the Light Railway was last used? (Note that it is possible that the whole length of the original hangar was not re-erected.

We can get some idea of the date of this picture in three ways.

Firstly, it would appear to be a fair time after 1945, since this is when TR5945 was transitioned into a lorry, and on close inspection appears to be in an almost derelict condition, with the tyres being completely bald. Before being shown this picture, I had not heard of it being used as a makeshift crane, which appears quite ingenious.

On close inspection, the top of the apparatus looks to be a post crane, as might be found on a recovery truck. This has been lashed to the top of two poles, having themselves been lashed together and planted on the bed of the lorry in a circular metal drum with a concrete base. The two main poles have been wedged into the base with wooden staves. It looks as if the whole thing is stabilized with guide wires secured in the ground.

Secondly, the office block and wash bay (white part of building in the picture) is complete, which from another picture (not shown) was being constructed in 1951.

Thirdly, it is known that this ex-hangar came from Ashford, Kent. The newspaper advertisement from the Uxbridge & Drayton Gazette 1953 shown below is likely to be for that same hangar for sale in Ashford.

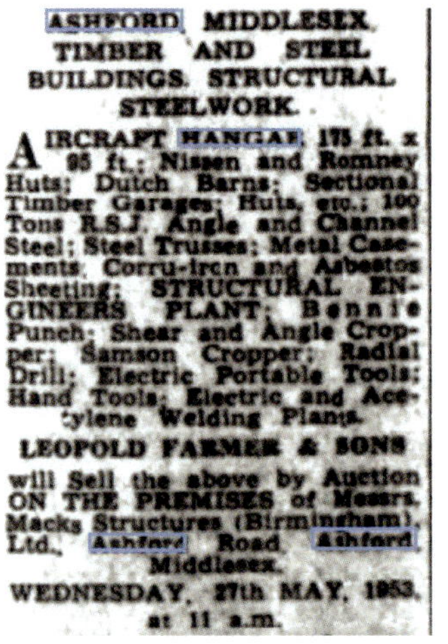

ASHFORD MIDDLESEX. TIMBER AND STEEL BUILDINGS. STRUCTURAL STEELWORK.

AIRCRAFT HANGAR, 175 ft. x 95 ft.; Nissen and Romney Huts; Dutch Barns; Sectional Timber Garages; Huts, etc.; 100 Tons R.S.J. Angle and Channel Steel; Steel Trusses; Metal Casements, Corru-iron and Asbestos Sheeting; STRUCTURAL ENGINEERS PLANT; Bennie Punch; Shear and Angle Cropper; Samson Cropper; Radial Drill; Electric Portable Tools; Hand Tools; Electric and Acetylene Welding Plants.

LEOPOLD FARMER & SONS

will Sell the above by Auction ON THE PREMISES of Messrs. Macks Structures (Birmingham), Ltd., Ashford Road, Ashford, Middlesex.

WEDNESDAY, 27th MAY, 1953, at 11 a.m.

So, most likely the picture was taken in the latter half of 1953/54.

I have not been able to locate a later map with the hangar addition shown, but assuming this was the hangar purchased, I have added a scale representation of the building which was 95ft wide. (It is possible that the whole 175ft length of the hangar was not used?):

A map of 1952 shows the main building, (in red) with the office extension (in white)

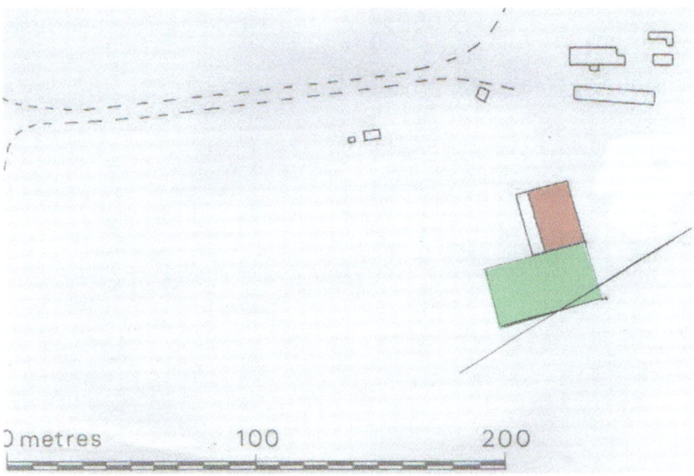

I have drawn in the aeroplane hangar addition in green, assuming that the hangar (known to have been from Ashford, Kent was that seen in the advertisement seen on the previous page).

This fits very nicely with Jack Parsons' account of the time he worked there in the 1960s, in which he says that the lines of the Light Railway crossed under the concrete base of the corner of the hangar.

The following two pictures are also of the hangar build.

(Both pictures Courtesy Jack Parsons)

Note the extremely bald tyres. Which suggest (but does not prove) that TR5945 was off the road by then?

THE RESTORATIONS

As most people reading this will know, there are three Silver Star buses that have been restored to their former glory and which regularly appear at Classic Vehicle meetings and bus rallies. These are the 1962 Leyland PDR1/1 Weymann Atlantean 1013 MW, the 1955 Leyland Harrington PSUC1/2 Tiger Cub (MMR552) and a similar model Leyland Harrington Tiger Cub (MMR553).

The first two of these were painstakingly restored by Old Portonian Jack Parsons, to whom, the people who can remember Silver Star owe a huge debt of gratitude.

I went to Gomeldon school with Jack and can remember vividly him coming into class with a detailed wooden model of a Silver Star Atlantean which he and his father I think had built from scratch.

Some of the history of MMR552 has been discussed earlier in this book and we have seen that by the early 1980s, the vehicle was gradually succumbing to nature and neglect. It was at this time that it was noticed by Ron Hayter, who made Jack Parsons aware of it. Jack and Ron acquired it in 1984 and Jack started on the restoration.

There are only a few pictures of the vehicle during the restoration and some of these are shown on the following pages. The first picture shows the old paint being stripped before inspection and repair of the alloy panels:

The previous picture is MMR552 getting etch primed following the restoration of the alloy body.

And here at Barton Park Eastleigh in October 1984 where it appears to be fully primed but there was no engine in it at the time.

And at a later stage, still in primer, but with the red paintwork already giving it its characteristic and instantly recognizable Silver Star good looks. The vehicle was moved to

The Red lion Car Park in Eastleigh for the rest of the restoration. The Red lion was owned by Ron Hayter who was the co-owner of the vehicle at the time.

To restore a bus from a disintegrating shell to a pristine roadworthy vehicle is a fantastic achievement, and for most would be satisfying, but as many will know, the enthusiasm that Jack Parsons had for Silver Star and their vehicles, led him to yet another project, and this time a much more daunting and challenging one.

Ex-Silver Star Atlantean 1013MW had for many years, like many other vehicles, been languishing in the yard of Berresfords' Motors of Cheddleton.

Jack had approached Mr Berresford several times with a view to buying the decaying hulk of this bus, but each time had been turned down, but on the death of Mr Berresford, he had placed a stipulation in his will that three of the vehicles including 1013MW should be sold for the purpose of restoration. Jack eventually bought the vehicle for £500. He made arrangements for it to be towed to the bus depot in Eastleigh where he worked and where he was given space for the restoration. Just to emphasise the enormity of the task, the following picture shows the bus as Jack first saw it in the Eastleigh yard.

The following pictures of stages of the restoration give a little idea of what a mammoth task this restoration was.

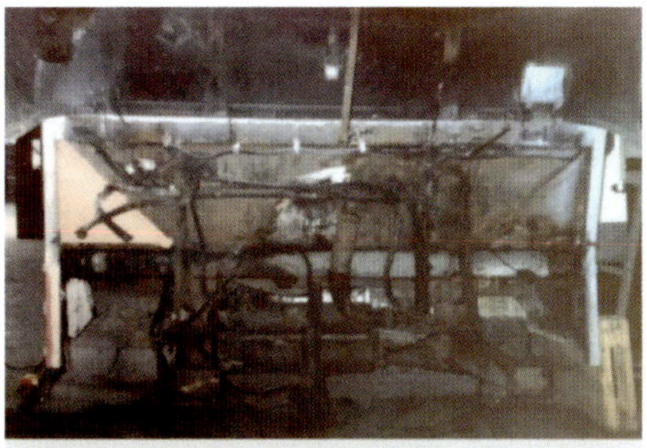
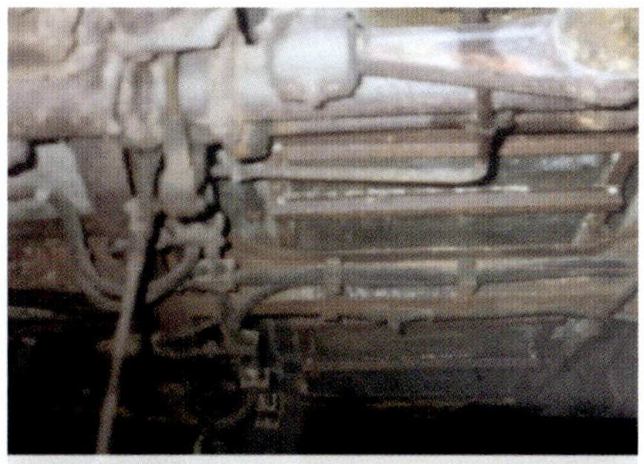
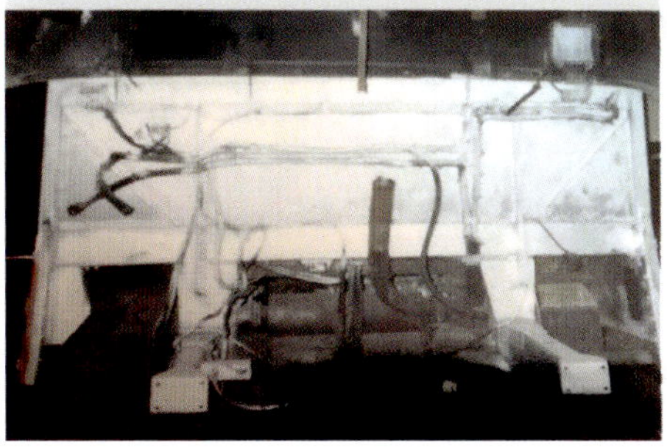

The engine which was in the vehicle was of little use, but fortunately, a suitable power plant was donated by James Freeman (Founder of The King Alfred group), for painting services he had previously benefited from. Some modifications had to be made to bring the engine back to its original standard. When the time came to repaint the bus, which would normally have cost thousands of pounds, there was another stroke of luck. In the depot, there remained a batch of paint from an earlier paint job on a luxury yacht, which just happened to be silver and red, and an almost exact match to the original colours. Such pieces of luck of course take nothing away from the skill, the other high costs and the sheer determination to get the project finished, when talking to Jack about the restoration, he told me that there was a lull in the project when he lost momentum for a while but that he fairly quickly got back into it until its completion.

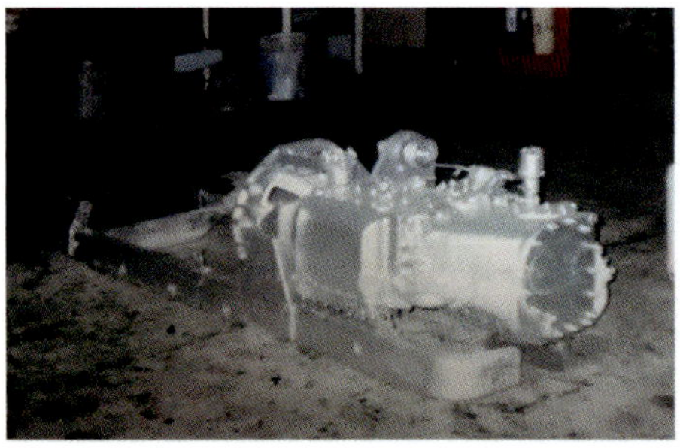

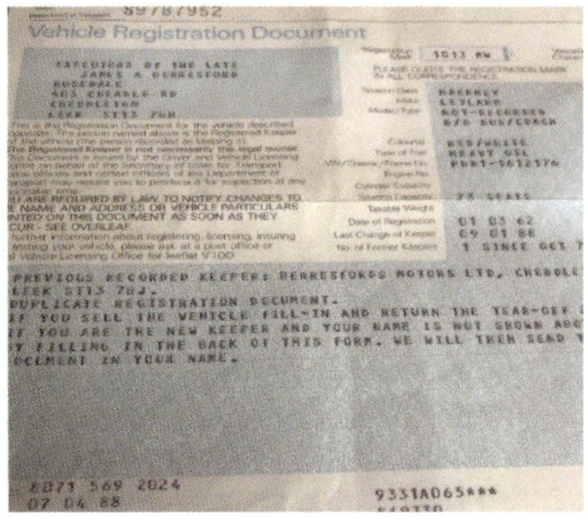

89787952

Vehicle Registration Document

EXECUTORS OF THE LATE
JAMES A BERRESFORD
1013 MW

YOU ARE REQUIRED BY LAW TO NOTIFY CHANGES TO THE NAME AND ADDRESS OR VEHICLE PARTICULARS PRINTED ON THIS DOCUMENT AS SOON AS THEY OCCUR - SEE OVERLEAF

LEYLAND
RED/WHITE
HEAVY OIL
01 03 62

PREVIOUS RECORDED KEEPER: BERRESFORDS MOTORS LTD,
DUPLICATE REGISTRATION DOCUMENT.
IF YOU SELL THE VEHICLE FILL-IN AND RETURN THE TEAR-OFF
IF YOU ARE THE NEW KEEPER AND YOUR NAME IS NOT SHOWN
FILLING IN THE BACK OF THIS FORM. WE WILL THEN SEND
DOCUMENT IN YOUR NAME.

07 04 88

9331A065***

An evocative picture of Jack Parsons driving 1013MW at its home, near the site of the former Silver Star garage at Porton Down during a reunion tour. I am told the MoD policeman allowed the picture to be taken on the condition that he appeared in it!

SILVER STAR MOTOR SERVICES

A time table has been kindly submitted for publication by the above Company for your special perusal should big ends and magnetos cease to function.

DAY NOT RUNNING	SALISBURY	ST MARKS CHURCH	CORNER	CORNER	IDMISTON	CAMP	ALLINGTON
N.S.	7 15am	7 19am	7 30am	7 35 am	7 40am	7 45am	-
N.S.	8 30	8-34	8 45	8 50	8 55	9 00	-
N.S.	9 0	9 4	9 15	9 20	9 25	9 30	-
N.S.	11 0	11 4	11 15	11 20	11 25	11 30	-
Sats	11 30	11 34	11 45	11 50	11 55	12 0	-
D.	12noon	12 4pm	12 15pm	12 20pm	12 25pm	12 30pm	12 35pm
Sats	1 0pm	1 4	1 15	1 20	1 25	1 30	-
D.	2 0	2 4	2 15	2 20	2 25	-	2 30
S.O.	3 15	3 19	3 30	3 35	3 40	3 55	3 45
N.S.	3 30	3 34	3 45	3 50	3 55	-	4 0
T & S	3 45	3 49	4 0	4 5	4 10	4 15	-
N.S.	4 0	4 4	4 15	4 20	4 25	4 30	-
D*	5 0	5 4	5 15	5 20	5 25	5 30	-
Sats	5 30	5 34	5 45	5 50	5 55	6 0	-
N.S.	6 0	6 4	6 15	6 20	6 25	-	6 30
D	7 0	7 4	7 15	7 20	7 25	7 30	-
D	8 45	8 49	9 0	9 5	9 10	9 15	9 25
D	10 0	10 4	10 15	10 20	10 25	10 30	-
Sats	10 30	10 34	10 45	10 50	10 55	11 0	11 10
D	11 0	11 4	11 15	11 20	11 25	11 30	-
Sats	11 30	11 34	11 45	11 50	11 55	12 0	-

N.S. Not Sundays.
Sats. Saturdays only.
D. Daily.
S.O. Sundays only.
T & S. Tuesdays and Saturdays only.
D* Not Saturdays.

This is a timetable for 1933 produced by Silver Star and submitted to Porton Camp authorities for publication in their newsletter. Note the humourous depiction of Policeman's corner and Targett's Corner. I note that at this time the bus from Salisbury stopped at Porton Camp prior to going on to Allington, which in latter years was reversed.

(Courtesy of Bourne Valley History Society)

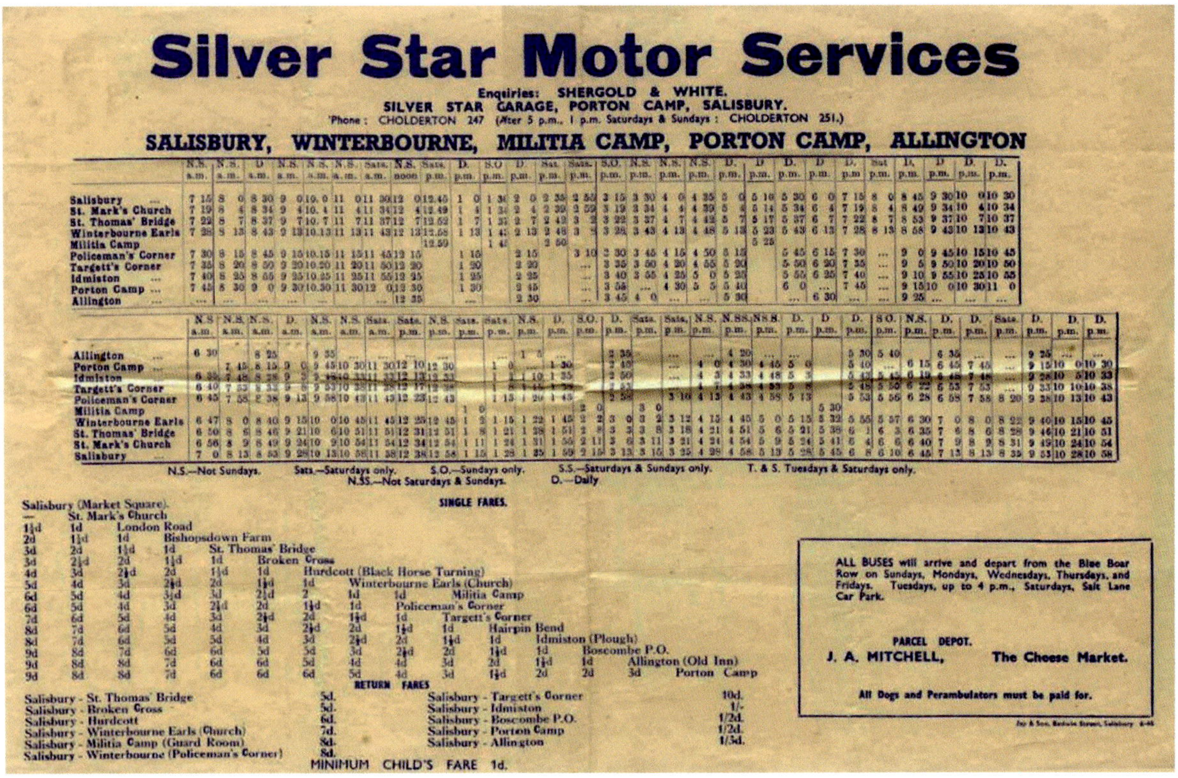

Silver Star Motor Services

Enquiries: SHERGOLD & WHITE.
SILVER STAR GARAGE, PORTON CAMP, SALISBURY.
'Phone: CHOLDERTON 247 (After 5 p.m., 1 p.m. Saturdays & Sundays: CHOLDERTON 251.)

SALISBURY, WINTERBOURNE, MILITIA CAMP, PORTON CAMP, ALLINGTON

N.S.—Not Sundays. Sats.—Saturdays only. S.O.—Sundays only. S.S.—Saturdays & Sundays only. T. & S. Tuesdays & Saturdays only.
N.SS.—Not Saturdays & Sundays. D.—Daily

SINGLE FARES.

Salisbury (Market Square).
— St. Mark's Church
1½d 1d London Road
2d 1½d 1d Bishopsdown Farm
3d 2d 1½d 1d St. Thomas' Bridge
3d 2½d 2d 1½d 1d Broken Cross
4d 3d 2½d 2d 1½d 1d Hurdcott (Black Horse Turning)
5d 4d 3d 2½d 2d 1½d 1d Winterbourne Earls (Church)
6d 5d 4d 3½d 3d 2½d 2 1d 1d Militia Camp
6d 5d 4d 3d 2½d 2d 1½d 1d Policeman's Corner
7d 6d 5d 4d 3d 2½d 2d 1½d 1d Targett's Corner
8d 7d 6d 5d 4d 3d 2½d 2d 1½d 1d Hairpin Bend
8d 7d 6d 5d 5d 4d 3d 2½d 2d 1½d 1d Idmiston (Plough)
9d 8d 7d 6d 6d 5d 5d 3d 2½d 2d 1½d 1d Boscombe P.O.
9d 8d 8d 7d 6d 6d 5d 4d 4d 3d 2d 1½d 1d Allington (Old Inn)
9d 8d 8d 7d 6d 6d 6d 5d 4d 3d 1½d 2d 2d 3d Porton Camp

RETURN FARES

Salisbury - St. Thomas' Bridge	5d.	Salisbury - Targett's Corner	10d.
Salisbury - Broken Cross	5d.	Salisbury - Idmiston	1/-
Salisbury - Hurdcott	6d.	Salisbury - Boscombe P.O.	1/2d.
Salisbury - Winterbourne Earls (Church)	7d.	Salisbury - Porton Camp	1/2d.
Salisbury - Militia Camp (Guard Room)	8d.	Salisbury - Allington	1/5d.
Salisbury - Winterbourne (Policeman's Corner)	8d.		

MINIMUM CHILD'S FARE 1d.

ALL BUSES will arrive and depart from the Blue Boar Row on Sundays, Mondays, Wednesdays, Thursdays, and Fridays. Tuesdays, up to 4 p.m., Saturdays, Salt Lane Car Park.

PARCEL DEPOT.
J. A. MITCHELL, The Cheese Market.

All Dogs and Perambulators must be paid for.

Silver Star timetable from 1946. Note the destination "Militia Camp", which I have only ever seen on this document, and obviously refers to what was previously known as Porton South Camp and more recently Winterbourne NBC(R) School. The term Militia Camp appears to be from WW2 and is still being used in 1946.

SALISBURY (Canal), WINTERBOURNE, PORTON CAMP, ALLINGTON.

Silver Star Motor Services.

	NS	NS	NS	S	S		S	NS	SO	NS	NS	NS	S	SO	NS	S	
	a.m	a.m	a.m	a.m	a.m	n'n	p.m	p.m	p.m	p.m	p.m	p.m	p.m	p.m	p.m	p.m	
Salisbury d	7 15	8 30	9 0	11 0	1130	12 0	1 0	2 0	3 0	3 30	4 0	6 0	8 0	8 30	8 45	10 0	..
Winterb'rne,,	7 30	8 45	9 15	1115	1145	1215	1 15	2 15	3 1'	3 45	4 15	6 15	8 15	8 45	9 0	1015	..
Porton Cp. ..	7 55	9 5	9 35	1135	12 5	1235	1 45		3 35	..	4 35	6 35	..	9 0	9 20	1035	..
Allington a	..	..	..	..	..	1240	..	2 35	..	4 5	..	..	..	..	..	..	..

	SO	NS	SO	S							S	S		
	p.m	p.m	p.m	p.m					a.m	a.m	a.m	a.m	p.m		
Salisbury d	1015	1030	11 0	1130	..	..	**Allington** d	..	9 40	..		..	..	..
Winterb'rne .	1030	1045	1115	1145	..	..	Porton Cp. ..	8 25	..	9 50	1130	1230	..	..
Porton Cp. ..	1050	11 5	1135	12 5	..	..	Winterb'rne,,	8 40	9 55	10 5	1145	1245	..	..
Allington a	..	..		..	..	..	**Salisbury** a	8 55	1015	1025	12 0	1 0	..	..

	S			S	NS	NS	S			S		S	SO	S	S		
	p.m	p.m		p.m	p.m	p.m	p.m	p.m	p.m	p.m	p.m	p.m	p.m	p.m	p.m		
Allington d	..	1 15	..	..	2 30	..	4 50	..	..	..	..	..	..	9 15	..	..	..
Porton Cp. ,,	1 0	..	..	1 25	2 40	4 45	5 0	5 0	5 30	6 0	6 45	..	9 0	9 25	9 30	..	..
Winterb'rne,	1 15	1 30	..	1 40	2 55	5 0	5 15	5 15	5 45	6 15	7 0	8 22	9 15	9 40	9 45	..	..
Salisbury a	1 30	1 45	..	1 55	3 10	5 15	5 30	5 30	6 0	6 30	7 15	8 37	9 30	9 55	10 0	..	..

N S *Not Suns.* S *Sats. only.* S O *Suns. only.*

Silver Star 1949 timetable. Note the Salisbury stop is in "Canal"

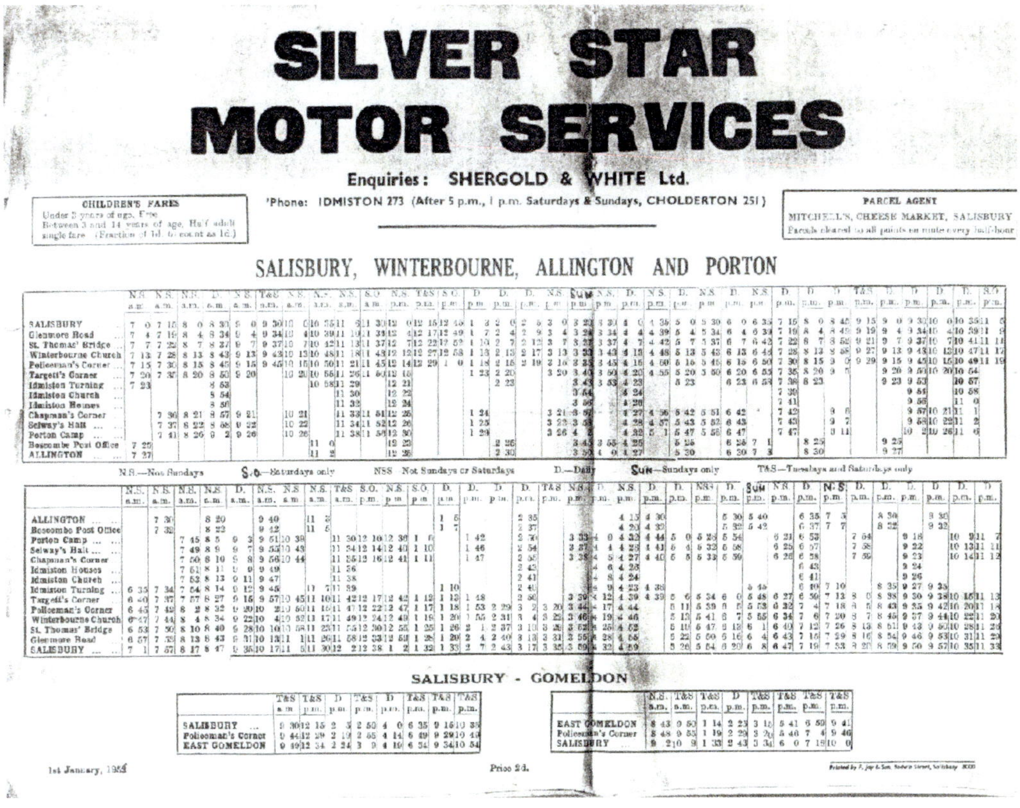

SILVER STAR MOTOR SERVICES

Enquiries: SHERGOLD & WHITE Ltd.

'Phone: IDMISTON 273 (After 5 p.m., 1 p.m. Saturdays & Sundays, CHOLDERTON 251)

CHILDREN'S FARES
Under 3 years of age, Free
Between 3 and 14 years of age, Half adult single fare (Fraction of 1d. to count as 1d.)

PARCEL AGENT
MITCHELL'S, CHEESE MARKET, SALISBURY
Parcels cleared to all points en route every half-hour

SALISBURY, WINTERBOURNE, ALLINGTON AND PORTON

N.S.—Not Sundays S.O.—Saturdays only NSS Not Sundays or Saturdays D.—Daily SUN—Sundays only T&S—Tuesdays and Saturdays only

SALISBURY - GOMELDON

	T&S a.m.	T&S p.m.	D p.m.	T&S p.m.	D p.m.	T&S p.m.	T&S p.m.	T&S p.m.
SALISBURY ...	9 30	12 15	2 3	2 50	4 0	6 35	9 16	10 39
Policeman's Corner	9 44	12 29	2 19	2 55	4 14	6 49	9 29	10 49
EAST GOMELDON	9 49	12 34	2 24	3 9	4 19	6 54	9 34	10 54

	N.S. a.m.	T&S a.m.	T&S p.m.	D p.m.	T&S p.m.	T&S p.m.	T&S p.m.	T&S p.m.
EAST GOMELDON	8 43	9 50	1 14	2 23	3 15	5 41	6 59	9 41
Policeman's Corner	8 48	9 55	1 19	2 29	3 20	5 46	7 4	9 46
SALISBURY ...	9 2	10 9	1 33	2 43	3 34	6 0	7 19	10 0

1st January, 1955 Price 2d.

Printed by F. Jay & Son, Salisbury

Silver Star timetable 1955

Silver Star Tickets

OUTINGS AND EXCURSIONS

During its forty years of existence, Silver Star, like many of the other companies, took advantage of its close proximity to the coast, providing seaside excursions to the seaside and other places of interest.

Photographs of these events are strangely few. I have included a couple of pictures earlier in this book of a couple of the companies' buses at the coast, and the following is all I could find.

Firstly, a picture of the Boscombe Working Men's' Club, gathered before boarding, what looks to be the Albion Viking bus (ML1862)

So, by looking at the fleet list it is possible to date this picture as being between 1927 when the bus was acquired and 1931 when it was withdrawn from service.

This picture is thought to have been taken at St Mark's Church Salisbury. Most of the group are wearing a flower buttonhole which may be significant!

The driver on the left is Ben White proprietor.

The second picture is of the arrival of an excursion at the coast.

And here, this rather wonderful picture of what, again, I believe is ML1862, the Albion Viking with an "All Weather" body by London Lorries Coachworks.

It must have been really good weather as the hood is down and only summer clothing visible. I guess the very slow speeds meant that it wasn't too draughty or perhaps they were just hardier than us?

The excursion has apparently just arrived at Clarence Pier, Portsmouth circa 1929/30. It appears the photographer has quickly alighted in order to take the semi-posed shot, no doubt then dashing off to a chemist to get the pictures developed and for sale on the return trip.

(Courtesy Frank Rhodes)

From the late 1920s/ early 1930s, we then have to jump to 1955. In this picture, a 10-year-old Mary Porter (Dixon) stands in front of Leyland JMR736 at Bognor Regis. The driver is Reg Bowley, and Mary's mother is sitting in the front of the bus.

(Courtesy Mary Dixon)

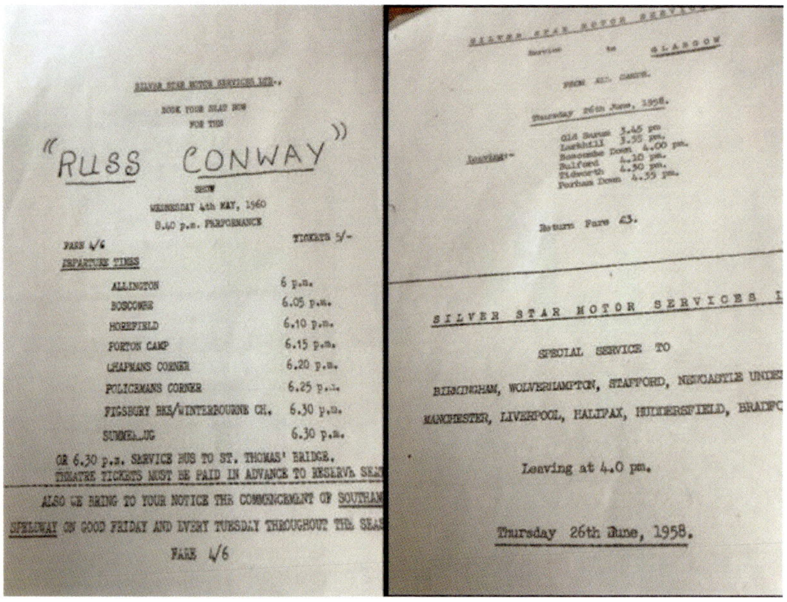

SILVER STAR MOTOR SERVICES LTD.,

BOOK YOUR SEAT NOW
FOR THE

"RUSS CONWAY"

SHOW

WEDNESDAY 4th MAY, 1960
8.40 p.m. PERFORMANCE

FARE 4/6 TICKETS 5/-

DEPARTURE TIMES

ALLINGTON	6 p.m.
BOSCOMBE	6.05 p.m.
HOREFIELD	6.10 p.m.
PORTON CAMP	6.15 p.m.
CHAPMANS CORNER	6.20 p.m.
POLICEMANS CORNER	6.25 p.m.
FIGSBURY BKS/WINTERBOURNE CH.	6.30 p.m.
SUMMERLUG	6.30 p.m.

OR 6.30 p.m. SERVICE BUS TO ST. THOMAS' BRIDGE.
THEATRE TICKETS MUST BE PAID IN ADVANCE TO RESERVE SEA

ALSO WE BRING TO YOUR NOTICE THE COMMENCEMENT OF SOUTHAM
SPEEDWAY ON GOOD FRIDAY AND EVERY TUESDAY THROUGHOUT THE SEAS

FARE 4/6

SILVER STAR MOTOR SERV
Service to GLASGOW
FROM ALL CAMPS.
Thursday 26th June, 1958.

Return Fare £3.

SILVER STAR MOTOR SERVICES L

SPECIAL SERVICE TO

BIRMINGHAM, WOLVERHAMPTON, STAFFORD, NEWCASTLE UNDE
MANCHESTER, LIVERPOOL, HALIFAX, HUDDERSFIELD, BRADFO

Leaving at 4.0 pm.

Thursday 26th June, 1958.

Another example of the entrepreneurial qualities of the Silver Star company. A trip to the Southampton Gaumont theatre in May 1960 to see Russ Conway. The 5/- ticket price would equate to ca £5 today. For a similar charge a return trip to Southampton Speedway. The proforma flyer, on which the name of the show could be easily written in by hand, suggests there were many such outings on a regular basis. Also, the flyer for the 1958 excursions to Glasgow; the £3 fee for the return trip, equating to ca £60 today (2021)

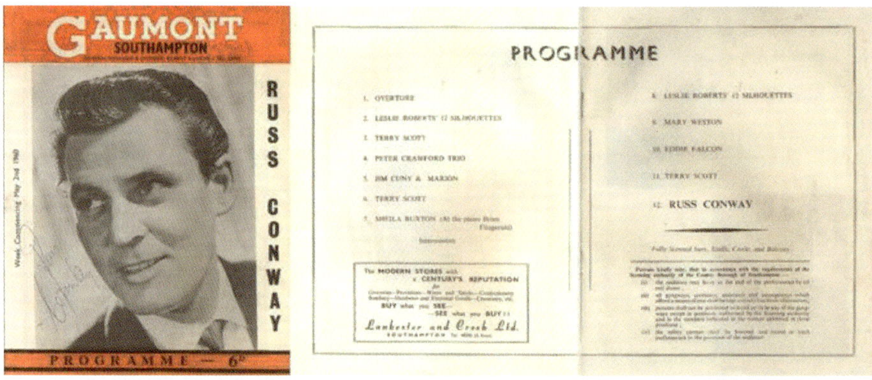

The May 1960 Russ Conway Brochure for that silver Star special shown above.

In circa late 1961 Or early 1962, Silver Star ventured further than it had ever been before, with a continental excursion. This was a tour of Germany with a group of Boy Scouts from Birmingham. The following pictures show XMW706, firstly in Idmiston proudly displaying "CONTINENTAL TOUR" as the destination. Note the AA badge under the destination, presumably for Continental breakdown cover? This picture although suggesting it might be on the first leg of the trip to Birmingham was in fact taken after the tour. Two small German badges in between the headlights confirm this.

Secondly, the vehicle is shown somewhere in Germany during the trip. A "GB" badge, which was a requirement at that time was attached to the rear of the vehicle, and this was still *in situ* much later when in the hands of Super Coaches of Upminster.

(Both courtesy of Jack Parsons)

(Courtesy Mike Walker)

Bibliography and Resources

Anonymous; *Silver Star Motor Services* (Local Transport History Library) 2015

Anonymous; *Motor 'Bus & Coach Proprietors of Wiltshire 1933* (republished by Roger Grimley) 2017

B1001 Body List, Thomas Harrington Ltd (The PVS Circle) 2012

Chislett, Steve; *Wilts & Dorset, 1915-95* (Stenlake Publishing) 2015

Carman, John and Garland, Kathy; *Coachwork by Heaver* (MDS Books) 2011

Carter, G B; *Porton Down: 75 years of chemical and Biological Research* (London HMSO) 1992

Daniels, Peter; *Around Amesbury in Old Photographs* (Alan Sutton) 1990

Dawkins, John; *Wilts & Dorset Buses* (Amberley) 2018

Morris, Colin and Waller, Andrew; *The Definitive History of Wilts & Dorset motor services Ltd 1915-1972* (Hobnob Press) 2006

Ride David; *In Defence of Landscape* (Tempus) 2006

Wiltshire, Andrew; *Looking Back at Independent Double-Deckers* (Bernard McCull) 2015

Industrial Railway Record March 1997

Appendix

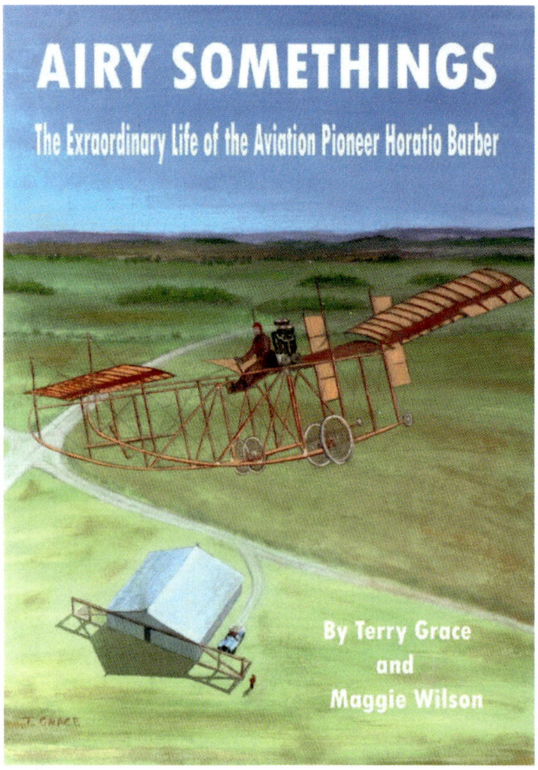

OTHER BOOKS BY TERRY GRACE

Horatio Barber is a somewhat forgotten figure from the pioneering days of "heavier than air" flight. Although well documented at the time, his considerable contribution to aviation is often overlooked in the history books. His achievements, if mentioned at all, tend to lie in the shadow of more famous aviators such as Cody, Roe and Sopwith etc. this book redresses the balance in that respect, and will hopefully put him in his rightful place in aviation history.

But there is much more, Barber had an exceptional life of peaks and troughs. We see him travel extensively across the world and involving himself in a variety of business ventures from fruit farming, through silver and gold mining, aeroplane design, construction and piloting. He was an author, insurance broker, hotelier and colonial development office r. Throughout, his businesses ranged from bona fide to unethical, to outright scams. Although a great self-publicist, he managed to keep most of his less-moral adventures out of the limelight; until now. (with Maggie Wilson) Available at Amazon.co.uk or Amazon.com

In the first half of 1909, an aeroplane shed appeared on a desolate part of Salisbury Plain known as Larkhill, in which an intrepid future aviator experimented with his prototype aeroplane. From these humble beginnings emerged a flying ground that was to become so important in the history of aviation. It was this aerodrome that helped eventually to persuade the War Office of the importance of the aeroplane in war, and which led to the establishment of an air battalion, then the royal Flying corps, and hence the Royal Air Force. This book charts the development of the site and its buildings, with special reference to the temporary sheds erected for the Military Aeroplane Competition in 1912, together with the siting of the more permanent sheds and how this was affected by the near proximity of Stonehenge. Available at Amazon.co.uk